Health Yeah

A Common Sense Approach to Mental Health

Sharla King

Copyright © 2021 Sharla King
All rights reserved
First Edition

NEWMAN SPRINGS PUBLISHING
320 Broad Street
Red Bank, NJ 07701

First originally published by Newman Springs Publishing 2021

ISBN 978-1-63881-353-8 (Paperback)
ISBN 978-1-63881-354-5 (Digital)

Printed in the United States of America

Acknowledgement

For the great loves of my life
My husband, Rex
And our children
Ryan and Jenifer
Regan and Laura
Cassidy and Casey
And saved the best for last:
Thank you, grands, for being yourselves. Cameron, Carly, Claire, Preston, Harper, and Bennett. P.S. The grands'—my happy place—pictures are scattered throughout the book.

For Cindy Berend and her precious family.
To one of the best friends I have ever had or hope
to have. Her smile is still contagious.
Cindy lost her long and well-fought battle with
the worst of the mental health diseases.
We continue to miss her.
Thank you and your family for sharing your lives with us.
Love you to the moon and back!

Contents

Preface	9
Introduction	11
Love	17
Marriage	21
Children and Parenting	26
Work	34
Joy and Sorrow	36
Stress and Depression	40
Feelings	47
Religion	51
The Good, the Bad, and the Ugly	53
Teaching	57
Aging	60
What I Have Learned	64
Positives to Consider	67
Rules for Being Human	68
My Absolutely—My Very Last Tip List	70
Good New and Old quotes That Are Actually True and Really Usable—or Isms	76
The Short List	78
Summary	80
Sources	85
Credits	87

Preface

Please allow me to introduce you to this book, booklet, pamphlet, or miniguide to hopefully get a handle on obtaining and maintaining your mental health. You, the reader, might be thinking *I've got a six-pack, can do one hundred pushups, run or jog four miles a day, and not even break a sweat!* Good for you; I'm jealous. But all of this strenuous activity may be taking place in the middle of a great depression or a mental breakdown.

Let's take a look at this from a different angle. You may be in elementary, junior high school, high school, college, applying for your first job, or filling out Medicare paperwork; and you are asked how healthy you are. You are the same person above that can do all of the strenuous exercising, so you answer, "I'm in good shape." You fail to mention that last week, you fell into that dark, deep well of depression, can barely lift your head off the pillow, but had to apply for this job today. So how mentally healthy are you today? And yes, I agree it can change day to day or sometimes minute to minute.

Almost everyone has one body perfectly constructed in the beginning in the womb (well, mine started out that way and then a few events have altered some of my parts, but I promise I won't bore you showing you all my scars!). You may be thinking *I thought we were going to discuss my mental health. We are!*

Right now, ask yourself this question, can I separate my physical body from my mental being? No, no, no. Of course, you and I cannot no matter how hard we try. The head, which entombs the brain, is still connected to the rest of the body!

Let's have a background check (for everyone!). Where are you mentally? How fit are you?

I would also like to say now that I highly respect and admire those of you who were born with less than perfect bodies—mentally and physically. I do believe a big majority of you have carried on with dignity and grace. I admire you greatly.

Did you know that the personal and social costs of mental illnesses are similar to those for heart disease and cancer?

Mental illness is treatable, not 100 percent but close!

There's no one-size-fits-all quick fix.

There's 20.6 percent of United States adults who experienced a mental illness in 2019 (51.5 million). This represents one in five adults.

Nearly one in five adults will have a diagnosable mental health condition in any given year.

By age fourteen 46 percent of Americans will meet the criteria of a diagnosable mental health condition in their life.

And, did you know that mental health illnesses can cost a lot of money? Think about *all* those billions trying to get fixed!

But did you know that, in this book, not only are we talking *prevention* but we will also offer tips and ways not to get fixed but to help minimize your issues (or whatever you call it). A disclaimer, I highly admire and respect the mental health professionals who work tirelessly to help people. I will ask you to go see a mental health professional or medical doctor if you have or will reach another level of a mental health condition. I do not discredit the professional field; they are necessary and needed for many.

Introduction

Just a few words about this person attempting to shed some good light on simplifying our mental health.

I am a simple, common, and, generally speaking, ordinary person—notice, I did not use the word *normal* as I believe that term is only a setting on a clothes dryer! And now, having said that, I could move to the extreme either way at the drop of a hat. You will notice many old sayings that I heard all of my life that I heard my parents say. I had no idea what most of the sayings meant at the time, but through my seventy-six years of living, I have finally figured out what most of them mean. I'm really happy because I have spent some valuable time trying to figure out some of the sayings.

And speaking of happy, that word could and should be the theme to this book. A good mental health recipe is "don't worry, be happy." You're thinking, *Easy to say, but.* We are going to go down that path of searching, finding, and maintaining a happy life. To give some examples, I asked our six grands to show in some medium their happy place. Their ages are seventeen down to three. Guess I'm showing six of my happiest moments of my life upon each of their arrival into my life. Those memories are forever etched in my mind and heart. All of you grandmas and grandpas know exactly what I'm talking about. Our six grands' pictures are scattered throughout the book. Enjoy!

I'm really just a simple girl: a baseball (or golf), apple pie, and Chevrolet kind of girl. I still cry a few tears as I place my hand over my heart and attempt to sing "The Star-Spangled Banner." I couldn't or wouldn't kneel if I wanted to with these ole arthritic knees! (Notice,

I said *ole*, not *old*!) Remember, no one is old. We are all just turning older every second that we are alive, and thank goodness.

I grew up on a small farm with both of my biological mom and dad and my sister who is seven years older. Our home was not full of money but better yet full of love. I went to the same country school from grades 1–12, graduated, and went to college. My dad and I got in the financial aid line, and, yes, I qualified. I knew it would be hard, but I was determined. And, obviously, it paid off because I got a degree. Actually, I got three degrees: my bachelor's, my Mrs., and my master's. I treasure all three, but I'm really partial to the Mrs. Almost fifty-three years' worth!

I majored in elementary education. I was sitting by all of my new friends in orientation, and the college people in charge told all of the education majors to get up and follow Dr. So-and-so. All of my new friends on my row got up and went, so I did too. I liked my major so much, I stayed in education officially for thirty-nine years—thirteen years of teaching and the rest in counseling after I got my master's somewhere in the mix. I got my master's in counseling with psychology as my minor, loved it so much, and have stayed fifty-plus years teaching and counseling. Guess I still like it, huh? (It could also be the reason I appear somewhat off balance sometimes?)

Oh yes, I taught one year while single, then married my college sweetheart Rex. I'm one and a half years older, and I'm still trying to raise him the way I want him! I'm a slow learner—I know, I know, one doesn't change 'em after one is married—but I guess it's still a work in progress. He says he is my biggest failure at using my counseling skills!

After seven years of marriage, we were blessed with twin boys. We always thought that God got tired of listening to us asking for a baby, so He gave us two and guessed He thought we would go away for a while. We did as we were very busy trying to raise those two, Ryan and Regan. Then, nine years later, He surprised us again with a little girl Cassidy, another beautiful blessing. We just thought we were busy!

I realize now why Ryan and Regan have become such great dads because they had so much good practice raising their sister. They did it all. They would even offer to babysit her so we could go on a date night. Little did we know that they would make her watch scary movies while we were gone (she just shared that with us recently!). So again, nothing is perfect! But they were good babysitters with just a few flaws.

I could have just sat and eaten bonbons all day and let the boys look after their sister, but I really needed to go back to work and counsel all of my other kids at high school. I had seven hundred, and I felt like Ole Mother Hubbard and I had all seven hundred in my shoe. And nobody better mess with my kids!

Our three kids grew up, went to college, met the love of their lives, married. And each has two children, and oh my, six fantastic blessings! Six grands, and are they grand? Just ask Meme. I do try really hard to look at others' pictures and be nice about it. Seriously, I still feel like I have a love and responsibility to and for every child, no matter the age. I think I'm addicted to all people's well-being.

As of this writing, I am still counseling "kids" at the senior level. I had to take a break during COVID. I am a senior, so I know exactly what they are going through!

Enough about my family and me. Let's cut to the chase. I hope to produce a shorter path to helping anyone and everyone who has any form of a mental health issue.

I do *not* have or even remotely claim to have all the answers to the vast depth of all of the mental health problems in the world. I feel sometimes we try to overload our brains with too much psychological language. (Sorry, Dr. B.) I work with a wonderful psychiatrist who is also my friend, and he allows me to pick his brain and expertise often and I do thank him so very much. He even tries to break it down on my level. I appreciate that.

My friend and colleague has also enhanced my stumbling through my psychological journey for the past few years. I have admitted my clinical side is lacking, and that is where she has been there for me. Often, in a stimulating discussion about depression, anxiety, or any mental health disease, she always fills in my clinical gaps, which is so helpful to me. She, like Dr. B, has been so gracious to share knowledge. I do have to say, only occasionally, that my experience and common sense theory came out on top in some of these discussions. Thank you, Becky.

I stopped my formal education when I received my master's degree in counseling with psychology as my minor, but I have the highest regard and respect for those who persevered and reached that highest level of psychiatry—psychiatrists and psychologists. I have many friends who are licensed professional counselors, counselors, and sociologists, etc. that do very good work.

I want you all to know that I highly respect all of these mental health professionals. They have and are working hard to earn their degrees. They are truly the experts. I have and am working hard to maintain my education in the mental health field. At this ripe ole age of seventy-six, experience and common sense are my best tools of the trade.

I hope by now you are a little or a lot interested in what's coming next. I sincerely hope that you gain some insight into what makes you tick. If I could figure that concept out for each of us, I would be a genius, and I know that's not going to happen.

So, are you ready? Let's move on.

And now, let's get started with some simple common-sense approaches that any and all can apply, use, and find helpful, I hope. It is my experienced opinion that every grown and semigrown person in the world has, is, or will experience some form of mental health problems or issues.

Of course, remember that there are many levels of each mental health problem. I would have said *disease* instead of problem, but many would say to themselves, *I don't have a mental health disease!* Call it what you want, but even those that say they are living the perfect American dream may be the worst of all, mentally speaking.

I remember talking to this sweet little older lady. She and her husband were approaching their fiftieth wedding anniversary. She told me that she and her husband had never had a fight. I was still a newlywed, probably celebrating fifteen years or so, and I began to think that my marriage was already on the rocks if you were not supposed to fight. Then I collected my thoughts and came to start thinking that that sweet lady was either confused, had forgotten, or that those two had had the most boring marriage ever!

My thoughts—everyone in the world needs a helping hand mentally at some point in their life! Forget the stigmatism! We can and should be able to talk about and discuss mental health: the good, the bad, and the ugly.

No, I did not call everyone (old term) crazy! I only said that sorta, maybe, sometimes we all could use some help—some more than others (you lucky ones!). And I hope the following helps some to realize it, or maybe you know someone that could use some help. This is a truth I have found to be so true. Most of the time I am doing any counseling with someone or a group of people, I seem to feel like maybe I might have gained more than the others. I guess I am lucky that I get free counseling from my clients. And oh yes, I always thank them!

Steps to everything

Everyone likes easy one-two-three steps for losing weight, happiness, more money, self-improvement, health, love, marriage, etc.

Some topics may take two steps; some may take ten. You get too many steps, we lose interest and don't follow all steps.

If I get too wordy, skip to the one topic and tips you are really interested in, and then later, maybe go back and pick up what you skipped. It won't hurt my feelings. I promise!

So here we go.

Love

What is love? I really like the St. Jude kids' definitions on the commercial. One said a puppy. Another said dancing, and one said to call the love doctor. They all seem to have pretty good insight. The question is pretty tricky. Love is not an exact science, is it? It is a topic that is questioned, sought after, ignored, tossed out the window, and most of the time, it is enjoyed by almost everyone in the world. But like everything else, it sometimes comes with its own problems.

The word *love* can be a noun, verb, adverb, or an adjective, a very versatile word and/or feeling. People, since man (or woman) was created, have tried to define the word and all that it means. I just thought of more kids' definitions from St. Jude: playing basketball with one leg or arm and playing the piano with no arms using their feet and toes. They worked long and hard to find the definition!

I hope that every baby born already is surrounded by love and nurturing, but I know that is not true. One of the saddest things in life is to not be loved from the moment of conception to your last day on earth.

If we did a survey or poll (being very popular lately), and I promise I will not get political, of one hundred dead people and asked their definition of love, we would probably get one hundred answers. You caught me; I'm going to poll the dead?

Well, I am just trying to make a point that there are many different views, ideas, and feelings about a very general and popular topic that is recognized worldwide. Many have tried to explain this intangible feeling: love is patient and is kind; is never having to say you are sorry (good movie, but I really never bought into that theory); caring; watching a beautiful sunset; snuggling your newborn; saying goodbye to your mom, dad, husband, wife, brother, sister, grannie, grandpaw, etc.; taking that last breath. Many will use their last breath to say I love you. By now, you are realizing the importance of this word *love*.

Every person in the world loves and/or is loved at some point in their life. Then why do we abuse, ignore, or deny love when it is an essential word or feeling or emotion?

There are many who have never known the ugly side of love. Pat yourself on the back. Congratulations! Yeah! Now, let's be honest. I know no one who has totally escaped the pains of love.

When I have been asked what my book is about, I have answered that it is like the CliffNotes of Mental Health, hence the book color. I know that all of my college buddies, including myself, loved our CliffNotes. No, it was *not* cheating. It was just another resource to go along with our in-depth notes taken in our classes!

As we all know, mental health is and can be very complicated. I remember trying to surf through mental health to obtain my master's degree. Many days and nights, I almost stayed in a fog. It is so hard to understand and decipher and to be as grounded in every topic as you can be. And then, one has to use their skills to try to help others round out their mental health issues. I suppose that is why I chose love as my first topic because forty-plus years of my career and working with many people, I have found that love really is what makes the world go round!

You will find at the end of each topic a few tips, suggestions, or plain ole common-horse-sense statements simply stated to help each of you "kids"—ages zero to one-hundred-plus years—hopefully get a handle on your mental health. I believe there is not a male or female alive in the world that couldn't use a refresher course on getting their acts or mental psyche back in shape even if you think they are "of sound mind."

Now, I remember one of my professors in Abnormal Psyche (already sounds scary?) class told me, "Sharla, you may become a good counselor, but also remember that you will never be 100 percent successful with everyone you talk with." I have always thought that if I reach or have reached one or more, then I will have been successful.

Tips on love

Make yourself lovable.

Love is a two-way street. You have heard, "To have a friend, you have to be a friend. Same goes for love and loving.

Sometimes, loving actions do speak louder than loving words.

Find your loving threshold. Everyone is capable of loving and being loved. Find your spot. Work on it.

Most of the time, *love feels good*—not 100 percent of the time but most of the time. It may take hard work, but it is worth it.

And remember, "It is better to have loved and lost than to have never loved at all."

Enjoy a good laugh with those you love and those who love you, maybe with those you do not know so well. They might not have anyone to laugh with.

Love often and *love* well. Get help to discover what blocks you from doing both. If you do not feel like you have healthy, good, intimate relationships, make changes now! Like any good health strategies, it may take some *work*, but it is certainly worth it!

Music—love it! A big believer in music, that's me. I almost said music therapy, but I might scare some of you off with the word *therapy*. My tastes in music range from crying-in-your-beer music to singing or listening to a good ole gospel song, opera, rock and roll, jazz, country or Western, oldies, etc.

Being a music addict, I really like it all as long as it has a good beat *and* no ugly words (I just prefer clean words! Ha!). A personal thought on one song about love from Johnny Lee's "Lookin' for Love in All the Wrong Places." We all seek love; and we can get distracted easily and end up in the wrong place, wrong time, and with the wrong person. Ouch! Go slow and don't rush things. There are many songs out there to help guide us, at least one song for every occasion!

Marriage

First comes love. Next comes marriage, and then... (We will finish this jingle in another topic.)

Yes, I know not every love relationship ends in marriage, and thank goodness. I do believe that there are more people who decide to marry than to stay single. And that is okay!

I also believe that a good marriage is built on several factors. Maybe the most important is to have a good relationship with each other. You and your friend really have to *like each other*. You say, "Well, I love him or her." That is good, but I mean, you really have to like even the way they smack their gum while chewing! I'm serious!

As silly as that sounds, the liking part might be more important than the loving part. I have observed many, and even myself, that it is easier to love someone than to really like them. Maybe the moral to this story is, on your first date, really watch your date, give him or her a piece of bubble gum, and then really observe how they chew or blow bubbles. Might be a game changer!

Just what all is involved in choosing Mr. or Miss Right?

Research indicates that love and positive relationships impact health and well-being. Statistics also tells us that happily married people live longer than singles and are healthier overall. There are lower rates of disease, including cancer and heart failure. (It may be why after a hard breakup, one may say, "My heart is broken.")

Stress levels are supposed to be lower in good relationships just because you have someone you can turn to for emotional support and advice. Holt-Lundstod states, "Positive relationships proved to be as beneficial to longevity as quitting smoking and exceeded the benefits of exercise."

Now those of you who are not in a happy relationship that might have even led to divorce may argue about your stress level. The higher a person rates their feeling of loneliness, the more likely they are to develop cognitive problems, with the loneliest twice as likely to develop Alzheimer's Disease.

Ever heard of oxytocin? It is a hormone that stimulates depression to make us feel good when we are close to loved ones. Also, it lowers stress, reduces blood pressure, improves mood, increases pain tolerance, and may help wounds heal faster.

Dr. Kathleen Light of the University of North Carolina at Chapel Hill found that people in *positive* relationships have higher levels of oxytocin, and the more physical contact one has, the more the levels seem to increase. Is that not a good reason to love and be loved more?

A study from Ohio State University showed that a married couples' positive support speeds up their bodies' ability to recover from sports injuries, including blisters!

This is my study. I looked at several reports from serial killers and people that have committed heinous crimes and murders. The majority of the perps had not been nurtured as babies and children.

Deprivation of touch stimulation in adults shows that many men become aggressive while many women become depressed and withdrawn. Are we going in a circle?

I certainly would be negligent if I did not mention everyone's relationship with their cell phones! Come on, fess up. It really is a pretty close relationship! I will say that peer pressure, business pressure, and every other kind of pressure you can think of is probably the reason you all have a cell phone. Oh yes, I have a cell phone too. Do I always have it glued to my hip? No. Just ask my kids or husband when they are trying to get ahold of me.

I know many people who are so proud of the number of contacts or friends they have on their phones. Is it really important how many one has or the quality of contacts? It probably is really okay, not a big deal. This rule applies to real people you see in person or can reach out and touch—quality versus quantity. I usually choose quality over quantity, unless it's a bigger piece of coconut pie sitting in front of me (hard to mess that up).

Social isolationists, listen up. (Why do we say up and not down? I have always pondered that.) Death rates are higher among people who are socially isolated. Numbers versus quality again.

We cannot ignore another type of relationship that can sometimes be even more important than a human being relationship, the pet population. Remember the quote, "A dog is man's best friend"? I have some friends that I know they would rather be in the company of their pet than with another human. I believe this to be worldwide.

Relationship loss is tough on everyone. Did you ever have your first love, at the ripe ole age of fourteen, dump you? Talk about hurt, sick to your stomach, aching, heartbroken right half in two, and all of the above at the same time—remember now?

I'm remembering that event in my life as I am writing, and I didn't even know what a relationship was at fourteen! Well, we all grow up, move on, get married, stay married or divorce, lose a spouse to death, or if you stayed single, your best friend dies. The loss of a relationship is tough. It can certainly mess with your heart and your mental health.

Aging is tough because you may outlive many of your relationships. That is why it is so important for one to develop and nurture good, strong relationships early in life so that when you do grow older (if you will notice, I do not use the word *old*; I try to use *older*). A person who is six is older than a five-year-old. A person who is ninety-six is just older than his ninety-five-and-a-half-year-old friend. Trust me, it's all relevant! You will start learning how to accept the loss of an older relationship. You know, all of that aging and maturity.

Tips or skills for maintaining good relationships, which equals good marriages

Disclaimer, you have all got to know that I do not 100 percent guarantee my words in this book; but please believe that these tips, suggestions, or ideas have been tried and tested and, in some cases, proven to work.

Trust. Long-term relationships are based on trust. We are more comfortable and relaxed and can be ourselves when trusted and are trusting. Find Shania Twain's song "If You're Not in It for Love" and listen to the words.

Acceptance. After learning about trust, we can be honest about our weaknesses. We have a shot at being accepted for who we are, no judging or criticism. What you see is what you get!

Support. We travel down the road of life with some planning and a lot of surprises. We slip out of our comfort zones often. We can either grow and become more, or we can punt. We usually have a choice.

A kind ear. When I was finalizing my master's degree in counseling/psychology, one of my professors told me he thought I would do okay as a counselor, but he gave me some advice that I have never forgotten. *Listen* more than you talk! My husband agreed with my professor. I'm still working on that skill fifty years later. Maybe I'll catch on soon. Venting is a very good coping skill, but one has to have a listener to be heard.

Understanding. In any good marriage or relationship, it surely helps when you *get it* when he or she says blah, blah, blah. They just know or you just know.

Someone to call on when you need a hand. Sometimes, we just need another pair of eyes or a set of ears on our project or when visiting the doctor.

Referrals and references. They can be a friend or foe, but more than likely, your mate or partner will be in your corner.

Share and celebrate. We all need to have a good or high self-esteem (not too inflated), but we need someone else to toot our horn louder. It just sounds more melodic!

Reduce stress. Anxiety causes stress, stress causes big problems. We all need some stress to be productive or get things done, but remember, don't sweat the small stuff cause it's all small stuff. And it will be if you let it be. We usually have choices!

Happiness and satisfaction. Having a good relationship usually means you sorta like each other. We can all LOVE each other, but in a really solid marriage or relationship, one has to like that other person.

Scripture says, "Do unto others as you would have them do unto you." It's a give-and-take deal. I realize the me-me-me syndrome has become very popular, but think about this a minute. Are you your happiest when all you do is take? Probably you are not if you are being honest. Give first, and maybe later, you will receive twofold. Also, giving does not always mean something monetary! How much does a smile cost?

Children and Parenting

This might be the most *emotional* topic that I will be putting my words to. Reason? This topic background and subject matter involves the thirteen most important, valuable, fantastic, beautiful, handsome, witty, sweet, kind, and intelligent people I have ever had the pleasure of knowing! Are you getting the idea of how much I love and care about my family? And that is my immediate family. I have one sister and brother-in-law, one brother-in-law and sister-in-law, all their kids, grands, and family; and I love all of our extended family very much also.

We are an incredibly close family, but not to the point that we get into each other's stuff, only if we are sharing happy, or if we are asked for advice. I will admit that I did not wear beige at either of our son's wedding, but I really do not look good in that color! I did try to keep my mouth shut in all of the preplanning. Do you know how utterly hard that was for me?

We do mention the hard or sad to each other but try to let each work it out on their own, but with many or few prayers just to give them a divine boost!

First comes love, then comes marriage,
next comes the baby carriage

See, I told you we would get back to it.

Babies, in my opinion, are truly a blessing. That would be my hope that everyone having a baby would feel the same. I'm not that naïve, but

I can hope. Having said that, I also realize that not all people have the same circumstances. I am a lucky mom as I had the best of the best support. Some people cannot have children or the choice to have children.

After seven years of marriage and several doctors later, we finally had our twin sons. We found out there were *two* at thirty-seven weeks! Did our world get rocked? On the way home from the announcement of two instead of one, my husband was very concerned that we or he had to come up with six names.

I'm about to faint over there in the passenger seat trying to grasp the fact that our one precious baby about to be born in three weeks had suddenly split into two babies. He is worried about six names! I will say that Rex went about his naming chore much more efficiently than I did.

The news of *two* babies that were coming soon put Mom into logistics mode. I immediately started thinking of how we would have to overhaul the one-baby nursery into, at least, a two-baby nursery. I said "at least" as the doctor also stated that one of his twin deliveries turned into three, as one was hiding behind the front one. I thought that was when Daddy Rex was going to go down!

We now needed two of everything. Simple, right? We lived in a small town up in the panhandle of Texas. Friends gave us a baby shower the week before the two-baby news. Lo and behold, every participant at the baby shower came by the house and brought a second of their original gift! We must have received one hundred onesies! What a good community of people.

I know all of you twin parents will relate in so many ways to the details of our first days of becoming parents. Obviously, all of the preparenting days was the easy part. I am sorry for those who had a rough pregnancy, both mom and dad. I know many of you did and are having it rough, but I will tell you that mine was almost flawless. Rex treated me like I was the queen of the king household, and to this day, of fifty-two-plus years. And I know that makes a difference. I know we can't go back in past times and make things different and better, but we can start today to make things better.

I know there had to be some very rough days having two babies, but honestly, I believe my God blessed us with forgetting the really bad or ugly. I mostly remember the fun and *happy* days. Then before we turned around, our twins turned nine. I was thirty-nine and holding *and* pregnant.

Yes, I turned forty two and a half months after our beautiful baby girl was born. Again, I had a great pregnancy, and our boys were so excited to be getting a baby sister. While still pregnant, they would sit by me and talk to her and argue about who was going to teach her to swim, ride her bike, etc. They were the best babysitters we ever had. Little did we know that they made her watch scary movies while we were gone on our date night! I literally could sit and eat bonbons while they played with her and took good care of her. Consequently, all three of our children are the best parents. How does this all happen?

Well, first, I hope I haven't painted a perfect picture because I just might have left out some of the bad or good or ugly. And there were some! I think we just chose to accept all and adjust to most of the situations that we were confronted with that might not have been our choice. (There are many.) We have to pick our battles to win the war!

All three of our kids are grown and married, and each have two of their own with the help of our two daughters-in-law and one son-in-law. Most of the time, I forget that they are the in-laws. I try to respect the fact that I did not birth them, but I can still love 'em as if they are ours too.

I cannot leave this topic without exploding all about our six grands. A friend rushed up to me in the grocery store to share and tell me that his first granddaughter was just born. "If I had known grandkids were this great, I would have skipped having kids!" No offense to his two daughters, he loved his girls beyond. He was just terribly excited about his first-born grand.

Now you will see some pictures throughout the book of my six grands. I asked them to come up with a picture of what makes them happy or show us their happy place. You will notice they range from seventeen to three and a half years old, so different mindsets.

I couldn't be prouder of each of our kids or grands. They are all so totally different; and that is what makes it fun, interesting, and doable. We all love, help, and support each other and have thrown in a fuss or two!

HEALTH YEAH

Parenting

Get it right from the beginning. Do not wait until your children are older and try to "fix" them, not that we give up and not try. We always keep trying! It is just easier to start at the beginning even before conception!

We had just gotten home from the hospital with our two bundles of joy. I was sitting on the bed crying. "I don't think I can do two babies."

Rex, with his infinite wisdom, looks at me and asks, "Well, which one of the boys do you want me to take back?" What a wake-up call for this new mom, me! He continued, "Well, get up and let's both get busy." And we did.

With our own three, being in the school system for seven years before we had children was a blessing. We learned so much from other teachers, coaches, and friends. I highly recommend anyone even considering having a family to plan on disciplining as much as loving from the first sight of that small, pink, squirming bundle you have just created! I was going to say that it turns out to be maybe even be 99/1 percent! But seriously, kids want to be disciplined. That is how we let them know they are loved.

In beginning a discipline procedure, we would tell each child that we always loved him or her, but we did not like their actions or behavior right then. It never hurt to throw in the classic my parents used to say. "This is going to hurt me more than it hurts you!" I really never believed that. We actually got more positive feedback with that approach.

You are right; this is not always easy. But no pain, no gain. You invest in your kids, and most of the time, the rewards are great. There will be bumps along the way, but all so worth it!

Tips—parenting and children

Some of these actually work!
Children zero to twelve years, always be ready for changes, surprises, knock-you-out-of-your-socks events daily, hourly, or minutely

(a word?). If you are older, can you believe you actually survived some of their childhood as the parent? Now you really do not remember vividly just how mad, angry, scared, sad, disappointed, or maybe heartbroken you were at the time. Thank goodness for time. Someone or something has a way to help us forget some of the bad or ugly details. If the previous did not happen, most would only have one baby!

And then, he or she turned thirteen—teenager. Before we go any further, for parents who have survived that seventeen-year-old—see, most of us have survived! Cain Spannagel, PhD, of Cane Reserve Western University tells us that positive reinforcement can work with teens because it works with all humans in general. We are all looking for it, the magic to resolve our teens. The tricky part with teens is finding what's most valuable to them. And, to add to the problem even more, maybe the adult in charge is more confused than the teen. They may still be searching for lots of answers. Houston, we have a real problem!

For some parents, "show me the money" might be a good tool. Like, show us a kid who doesn't like money. Actually, show us any living human being that doesn't like money!

The three big tools for parents are (l) touch, (2) talk, and (3) look. With your babies, you held them, talked to them, and looked at them. Did you stop with the three main tools and why? Your teen still craves your attention. The goal is to be physically and emotionally present for them in whatever way they will allow you. Being there will help reinforce the behaviors you want. Whatever you offer needs to be honest praise. Kids see through. It is important to praise even small acts of behavior that they have control over. They might repeat it. Instead of being critical of your teen spending too much time online, ask them to teach you something they enjoy online.

Include your teens' friends. Respect your kids' relationships, or you might help them see that maybe it's a bad choice. Positivity with a teen goes a long way.

Bribery—pay 'em off—might work for some, but most research shows that they get the money and maybe decrease the motivation and go back to the old habit. The impulse to do well is not linked to the nice feeling they got to get the money.

Love your kids and as many others as you can. Remember, it does take a village to raise a child.

Discipline, we used to call it tough love. Still my opinion, we need to go fifty-fifty of love and discipline.

Lead. You are the adult. Until your child is out of your home and on their own, and even sometimes past that, you, the parent, should be the go-to. I have seen very few pals or BFFs parent-kid relationships work and not for long. Leave the besties thingy for you and your spouse.

Listen. When your child, teen, or older wants to talk, you *listen*!

Read. Read to your baby and/or your unborn. It is never too soon to start. Read and continue to read to them maybe as they are walking out the door on their way to the prom! Reading with the kiddos is a bonding experience, is educational, and has proven to be an IQ enhancer.

Last tip for children or parenting of any age—drumroll

Grab your hat. Hang on.

This too will pass!

Honestly, try to enjoy as much as you can. Capture many memories because you wake up one morning and that sleepless baby you were up with all night, teething maybe, will be a teenager; and the next thing you know, that teenager will be thirty years old. Enjoy, enjoy!

P.S. tip. You, the parent, mostly tell the zero to twelve child in your talk. You are teaching, grooming, and nurturing. Occasionally, you allow them to ask questions—question your rules for clarification and/or state their side.

Thirteen and up, I left teens unended as some sorta-grown people still act like teens. That's a joke, not a very funny one to deal with.

It is very nice when you reach that time in your teen's life when you can *talk* instead of always *telling*. I think the teen gets ready for that big day too. You will probably both know when that time arrives, and you can both breathe a sigh of relief.

HEALTH YEAH

Work

Why would I throw in a topic called work? Think about how work or the lack of work impacts your life. Either scenario has probably brought you several problems. And, not to leave a group out of the wonderful world of work, there are those who work hard at not working. I am not even sure how to address that group. I am pretty sure there is a larger majority who try to stay gainfully employed. So *work* is a very important topic.

If you are the low man or woman on the totem pole, you are constantly trying to move up, and enter a certain stress level. If you are employed but treading water (not moving up or down), with no promotions or raises, you may feel that there is no gain or you feel stymied, bored, or have no satisfaction in your work. If you are the supervisor or boss, others may think that you have it made.

The truth may be that the boss is scared of failure, with not enough production and no big money coming in, etc. And remember, when you are at the top, everybody is shootin' at you! (And hopefully not literally! Also, remember, gun sales have skyrocketed this year.)

So at every level of work or no work, there can be many problems. We cannot usually discuss work without connecting money to it. Speaking of money, I love it. Or I will say, I like it a lot. Who doesn't? As much as I like to have some extra money, I will share this thought. Money truly is the root of all evil (and some good).

Come on. Try to think of two or three things in your life where there is not a dollar sign connected to it. Hard, isn't it? Didn't think you could. So again, work or money is very important. Can't live with it, can't live without it!

I am sure that there has been a study on people who have gone bankrupt and ended up needing professional help. I do know people who have lost their minds because they lost their fortunes or their minimum-wage jobs. Both are equally important. Before you attack me, I see much value in all honest work, big or little jobs. Again, we all have choices, and sometimes, we have good or bad luck in our work situation.

Tips

Be proud of the choices you have made in work situations or careers. We do not always get it right the first time, but keep working at finding your thing.

One of my professors in college told our class that the average person will change majors in college and/or in their lifetime of work an average of seven times. See, that definitely proves once again that "average," I am not. I'm in maybe my number-two job in noncounseling or teaching. Seven changes sound like a stretch to me, but then I do know that number doesn't come even close to some people I know.

Most every person in their work or professional life will quit or lose a job. You get furloughed, laid off, get fired, or you resign to try to find yourself! Some people are still looking. Some jobs do not pay very well and can be a tough job for some. Try to remember you are not a complete failure if you are attempting to correct a difficult situation. Keep on trying.

Try to develop good work ethic. Some traits of good work ethic: (1) honesty and integrity, (2) show up on time, (3) be a team player, (4) loyalty, and (5) an attempt to live the American dream.

Maybe the most important tip for this chapter—pursue a career in something that you really like and are happy doing. Being a happy camper at work will definitely help you to be an all-around happy person.

Joy and Sorrow

What is the ultimate goal of every person in the world? Okay, okay, I think you are right. Most people will answer, "To be rich," plus maybe successful or famous. Maybe the age factor factors in. I am sure that when I was twelve, I wanted to be a movie star, a rich one, and live in a mansion.

Obviously, at seventy-six, my goals have changed somewhat or a whole lot. Now when I start contemplating life and my goals, the daily goals are to be healthy and happy, and I use my plan in my head for all my family and friends. I try not to reveal the plan unless they ask to hear it. I have found that is a good rule to follow.

Funny how a few years change our priorities. Now being in education for fifty-plus years—or is it a one hundred years?—I have known some twelve-year-olds that shared my goals, and they reached those lofty goals. I have always been somewhat of a dream-big kind of a girl, not so much for myself but for our children and all of those children in Mother Hubbard's shoe.

When our daughter was in high school, she seriously started looking at the medical field. Being anxious to help her and guide her, I discussed her endeavors with the military recruiters. They were happy to recruit her and send her to medical school, but she might have had to spend some time on the battlefield dodging bullets. She declined their offers and has become a very successful nurse practitioner on her own. I had really elevated her in my mind. My goals? I was seeing her becoming the surgeon general!

Our sons, we knew, would go to college the same moment; so we also knew we would need double tuition. My researched plan was to let them go to Alaska and work on a fishing boat in the summer. Why, they could each make a year's tuition in one summer!

If they lost even one little finger in the fishing career, it might have squelched their goal of playing college golf! I didn't think of that! So they too declined the fishing boat job, went to college *and* played college golf, were very successful with all twenty of their fingers, still enjoying the lifetime sport of golf, and have been hard workers ever since!

Finding joy and happiness is a very individual endeavor. Most of the time, we cannot make it happen for the other person. We can be a catalyst or an adversary for another, but it still pretty much has to come from each individual.

The opposite of joy is sadness or sorrow. It almost makes me sad to even have to address this topic, but it is reality, a fact of life. Not many people I know try to be sad and maintain that lifestyle—some really do—but sorrow or sadness just kinda jumps on us. It blindsides us. It sneaks up on us when we least expect it, and then we have to go and deal with it!

We have all met or known someone who goes around with a smile on their face 24-7: always happy, cheerful, never a frown to be seen. Do you trust them? Do you really like them or even think they are for real? Probably not!

Now there probably are some of those people that are real; yes, I'm sure of it. This reminds me of a story of this really sweet little lady approaching me. We were talking, and she told me that she and her husband had been married over fifty-five years and never had a fight! At that time of my own marriage, I'm thinking that they must have had a very boring marriage! (I felt this story was worth repeating.)

Obviously, the most legitimate reason to be sad or full of sorrow is the loss of a family member, a friend, job, pet, an unwanted event, promotion, demotion, bad gossip, lies, etc. There could be many more reasons. I would not even attempt to try to persuade one to take *it* all with a grain of salt, smile, and move on.

There are deaths and losses of all kinds that need to be grieved. And is there a time frame for grieving? No, no, no! There could be some parameters, but it can be totally different for each of us. Never assume that when Aunt Susie lost Uncle Fred that she should *be over it* in your time frame. We all can mourn and learn to cope, but we also can never expect someone to forget their loss.

Tips

Learning to cope with any of your mental health issues can sometimes be overwhelming, but it is also very much needed. If your sorrow, sadness, or negativity has taken over every area of your life, *stop*, take a good look at yourself, and let's develop a plan for regaining your *positive* self. I didn't say you have to totally forget. You might just need to accept and adjust! Or try to tweak your grieving or negative attitude.

If left on its own, you and your body, heart, and soul could go into a depression, another topic to be discussed later.

Coping equals (1) taking control, (2) learning to meditate, (3) seeking out support, and (4) managing your stress.

Change. Everything changes. Even change changes, yet some things stay dismally the same (ole Arthur*itis*). You are human. Pick your battles to win the war.

Change what you can change, and accept or embrace the things you cannot change. Especially all of you perfectionists out there, you could go totally off to perfection land—that is not good or perfect!—and be lost forever. Maybe concede just a little, or some call it compromise. And try to embrace or enjoy some of the changes forced on you. *Shock*—you might even really like the changes. Hard to admit! Just don't share your happier thoughts with your critic. Surprise them with the new you!

Must *change* involve moving negative to positive? I had a very hands-on experience in my forties. After a near-death illness that lasted for about a year, the move from negative to positive happened about midyear. As soon as I started taking things in, digesting where I had been and where I wanted and needed to be, and with much family and friend support, I began to move to the *positive* side of life.

The Man Upstairs convinced my sometimes hard head that it was not my time to go! I thought I had a chance to live, and I took it and worked on it. A positive attitude will take you a long way!

If you are a born pessimist, well first, I am so sorry. Please try this.

Don't despair.

Look deep. Wow, do I need to change?

Question yourself, is change possible?

Stop or interrupt your negative thoughts. Self-talk yourself out of your old way of thinking. Hey, my glass really is half-full! Feel better?

Well, now that we have everyone accepting all of these changes coming our way and everyone has a very positive attitude, we can all take a deep sigh of relief. Come on. Breathe deep to the count of four through your nostrils and out through your mouth slowly to the count of four.

Actually, take three of these breaths, and you will feel like a brand-new person or at least very much relaxed. I usually feel like a puddle of melted Jell-O after deep breathing!

Hey, I didn't tell you that I am an ole medicine man or a cure-all. This mental health stuff is kinda complicated. I am just trying to simplify some of it and give you some very cheap aids and tips to help yourself.

Did the deep breathing exercise cost you a dime or even a penny? That's what I thought.

Stress and Depression

Stressed spelled backward is desserts, one of my favorite things in life. Now do not get me wrong; do not totally disregard the importance of stress. We all need or require some stress! Yes, you read right. When you have been your most stressed out—remember that worst day of your life so far—you would not agree with me.

Look above where I said we *all* need *some* stress. Some of us abuse the quantity level! Let's put it this way. If some of us did not have some stress, we or they might not ever leave their bed or couch. Have you ever been called a couch potato? They might get the award or trophy for best-destressed person or the best of the best couch potato.

Now, I can enjoy my recliner with the best of 'em; but on those days, I feel like a slug, snail, or pure worthless as for being a productive citizen. I really do believe we all need some stress. It makes us productive, but come on, really?

Now we will address the group that tends to overdo it with attempting to be superman or woman. These super productive people saturate their mind, body, and soul with as much stress and drama as they can possibly afford or can hold up to, they think. Houston, we have another problem! (And I am not sure whom to give the credit for this statement. NASA?)

I agree that some people really thrive with an abundance of stress, and they can be very successful while having a nervous breakdown. I hope not all do.

Do we agree that we all need some stress? Do we agree that too much stress is *too much*? Do we agree to try to hit that *happy, healthy* middle? When I start discussing my middle, it really scares me. For years, I have had to watch my middle expand and expand, and well, you get the picture. Now I am pretty comfortable in my own skin, so actually, I'm enjoying my physical and mental middle. This is a different middle. We could be slightly addressing the bipolar issues now under this depression topic. You know, they are all tied in together in some way.

I like to compare my mental middle to a car and the gears. I actually know very little about cars and how they run. I have always thought you put gas in them, and they are supposed to go. Now, I understand a little about the gearshift. There's park, drive forward, back up or reverse, and *neutral* or idle.

Neutral in a car is like our mental middle. When one of us gets our mind set into our mental middle, it is like the neutral in our car. We can sit idling while we make choices about going forward or backing up. If we can try to keep mentally balanced in our middle or neutral, then it will be easier to enjoy the fun and happy going forward.

If we feel balanced mentally in our middle or neutral, when the bad or ugly, sadness, sorrow, or anything that tends to bring us down or spiraling in the downward direction, we will have a better chance to deal with the bad, ugly, depression, or any negative feeling. Remember, our best and maybe shortest coping skill is to accept and adjust. Time required to accept and adjust might make it the longest coping skill! Everyone reacts differently.

I think I have already stated that I firmly believe that we cannot separate our physical self from our mental self. We all come as a package deal. We've got 'em both, so there, gotta deal with both. I have thought for years, and some of you have too, *Well, as soon as I lose some weight, I'll quit being so stressed out.* So how did that work out for you? At my current weight, I'm somewhat concerned that I have lost too much weight. Go figure; we are never happy! I need to practice what I preach.

Oh yes, the happy middle. Where is it? We all enjoy a party. You know, balloons, cake, ice cream, a few adult drinks, flowers, etc. I used to party with the best of 'em. Today, maybe an hour, and I'm toast! But I still enjoy that high. Then the opposite comes along. You or I start feeling as if we are spiraling into a deep, dark well—that deep dark well called depression. It is all I can do to say, much less put that word into print. From here on throughout the rest of the book, I will simply use the big letter D.

Hopefully, not all of us will hit the very bottom of that deep, dark well. It is scary and lonely and just not a good place to be. I have been there temporarily, thank goodness. I was blessed to be able to pull out of it; many are not. My point, let's all strive to pull up out of the well and pull down from the euphoric party and get to our happy middle. If and when you can get to your middle, then work on maintenance. Again, please feel free to use all the *free stuff* (tips found at the end of each chapter).

I would feel very remiss if, before I leave this topic of stress—we never really leave it, do we?—I must say a word or two about PTSD or post-traumatic stress disorder. Civilians can have PTSD also, but the group that immediately comes to my mind are our vets and our active military.

How I love 'em! The sacrifices they each and all have made and are making for every one of us Americans is immeasurable, and for their families too. I love and respect each of you and those who have gone on before us. I have the same sentiment for our firemen/firewomen and police (all-inclusive) officers, all medical personnel, and any other first responders that serve unwaveringly.

These people sign up for these jobs to *help* other people. Wow! How unselfish. I cannot even imagine the combined stress of all of these people. And yet again, I hope maybe just one of our statements in this book might put a smile on a face or maybe even a good ole belly laugh!

Obviously, I do not have a quick fix for PTSD, or it would have already been tried and would have fixed everyone suffering from this disease. Hopefully, some or maybe just one of my tips will help. Tips are at the end of chapters and at end of the book.

The word *stress* is big in the psychological world. I remember it vividly entering my professional world—to really know and understand what it really is and what comes from it—when I served my first year as a high school counselor. I am sure that that sweet fifteen-year-old girl sitting in my office sobbing had no idea what kind of professional feelings and scary questions she awakened in me as she said in my office, "Mrs. King, I am so stressed out. I think my world is crumbling. Please help me. I don't know what to do. I'm just so stressed."

First, I knew some of the girls' academic record and accomplishments. She's cute as a bug, and she was dressed in the normal trend of the day. I was thinking prematurely, *What in the world does this sweet thing have to be so stressed out about?*

Then came the outburst. "John Smith"—I never had a student named that. See, still licensed to confidentiality!—"just broke up with me!" Even quicker on my part, I had to quit thinking, *Well, that's silly. You will have a new boyfriend by noon.*

To finish up with that conference, I believe I helped dry her tears, offered some alternative solutions, and she went on her way. And I do believe she had another new boyfriend soon. Might not have made it by noon! The good point that I learned, everyone's problems are *big* to them at the time. Do not diminish them. Turn my counseling hat around and *rally*! Try to help and not embarrass anyone. It could be you or me needing help from that fifteen-year-old someday. Paybacks can be hell!

I also learned to never make someone, kid or adult, feel that their problem was or is petty or insignificant. She came to see me for help or advice, not a lecture on her no-good boyfriend (she probably ended up marrying him). After she slowed up with the tears, we both talked and shared some feelings, and eventually, she smiled a time or two. I might have even got in my one-liner. "There's always more fish in the sea." I always wondered if she knew what that line meant. Sometimes, mostly, there is not a very good follow-up program or survey in school counseling!

Now, I did not try to *fix* her problem, which is what every client or counselor wants; but instead, most counselors try to offer a plethora (love that word) of solutions. I think of solutions, then let them choose and hopefully make a good choice! Sounds simple? Sometimes, it really is. Whew!

Well, I have told you some of my first dealings with stress and now the big D. Remember, I told you we would refer to depression with just a D. I don't even like the word. It represents so many different feelings for everyone that has been D'ed or has D'sion or will have D'sion. I would dare say that D is the Cadillac of all mental health diseases, or maybe I mean it is the most common for most. I have worked in several mental health settings other than the public schools, and by far, D is the most diagnosed disorder in my work environment.

I sometimes call D a sneaky snake. It kinda sneaks up on you without you even being aware that it is in your neighborhood. You can be having a pretty good day or night, and *wham*, it hits you like a ton of bricks out of nowhere! Surprise, surprise, before you know it, you have just fallen into that deep, dark well all the way to the bottom. You look around, and there is no ladder or rope or steps out of there. Some choose to sit at the bottom. Most choose to holler for help, and the work begins.

Some have described D as a prison, and what are the chains of D made of? These chains have been called irrational guilt, fear, shame, being unable to love, and/or being unable to forgive yourself or others (partial list).

One of the side effects of D that is not at the forefront of D is a low self-esteem. Low self-esteem is a real bummer. What isn't a bummer that's connected to D? This low self-esteem is more like a dog chasing his tail backward—going in circles. The lower your self-esteem is, the more D'ed you are. The more D'ed you are, the lower your self-esteem is. Go figure.

Do you believe that sometimes you can be your own worst enemy? Actually, we can talk ourselves into or out of some very good or bad situations or thoughts. Either way, it is called self-talk. Science tells us (sound familiar recently?) that we probably run over a thousand thoughts through our heads every day or night in a twenty-four-hour span. Now, if we allow even 50 percent of those thousand thoughts to be negative, we have a pretty good chance of becoming D'ed unless you have a strong will and can adapt quickly to the positive side.

When you have a battle of positive-versus-negative plan going in your head, you had better hope positive prevails or wins. Negative will lead you down a rabbit hole you do not want to go to. Negative only breeds more negative. There is usually light at the end of the tunnel if you keep looking!

We mentioned earlier about striving to get to our middle physically and mentally. To me, this is about as good of an analogy as I can provide about D. Now, I love a good party as much as the next guy or gal. I could hang with the best of 'em. At seventy-six, my hang time has diminished. Maybe a good thirty minutes to an hour, I'm out. I'm done like a steak. I'm toast. I'm ready to go home and get a good night's sleep. I usually enjoy my big thirty-minute night to the max. Get all I can, enjoy it, and call it a night! You know, cake, flowers, balloons, good friends—I'm in.

The next morning I might get up, eat breakfast, trying to start my new day that has been provided. Uh-oh, the big D comes calling out of nowhere. It catches me totally off guard, and I don't even know why. I find myself falling 'til I hit rock bottom of that deep, dark well. There is no rope in sight. I'm scared, angry, frustrated, afraid; and I don't even know why.

While trying to make some sense of my feelings, I remember: get to my middle, my safe ground or zone, or comfort zone. We all want to feel comfortable in our own skin because the skin on your back is the only skin you have in this game of life!

Every human being is unique! There is only one of you. Some of you will say, "Thank goodness." Each person on this earth has one body, one mind, and one spirit. You own it! Please take care of it physically, mentally, and emotionally. Are you going to hit roadblocks or hurdles? Oh yes, many will come your way. Think about your past, present, and what the future may hold. So what do we do? We try to go over, under, around, or through each of them. If at first you don't succeed, try and try again.

D is one of the biggest and usually most expensive hurdles you will come across. Did I just mention money? How many dollars are spent trying to combat this disease?

Here are some signs of big D: change in eating habits, a loss of any kind of interest in people, feeling tired all the time (no energy), and thoughts of death or suicide (a few words on this later).

Tips

Do some quick exercises.

Schedule a massage, or you can massage your own feet and hands.

Dance. I have found myself dancing in my den when Rex is gone, or he would be dancing with me! On our patio, there is a sign that states, There's always a reason to dance. I totally agree.

Knead and bake bread. Go ahead and pound that dough. Release something.

Stretch yourself and/or put a rubber band on your arm. Pull out and let go. The sting might shock you into a different mood.

Meditate. Come up with your own place or time.

Read a good book and get lost in it.

Clear the mental clutter from your head. Sometimes, we overload our thinking!

Four fundamentals to manage stress: eating well, getting enough sleep, being active, and maintaining social interaction.

Find your neutral.

Feelings

This chapter on feelings almost did not make the cut. Maybe there is not enough written or said or thought about feelings in general. And then, it was almost like the lightbulb came on. Follow along with me here.

I make an appointment to see one of my doctors. I go in and get called back (obviously pre-COVID days!). The doctor comes in, sits down at his computer, and may or may not have looked up at me, and he/she asks, "How are you feeling today?"

Of course, we need to address feelings. We all think and talk about our feelings nearly every day. One can go off in so many different directions with this topic.

As stated earlier, every human being in the world is unique—a very positive statement and is meant to be because you cannot argue about that.

All of you with low self-esteem, please latch on to this statement and believe it. Now when one of your buddies tells you, "You are one of a kind, and thank goodness they threw away the mold." Please do not get too offended, and just know they really are kidding.

Being a very unique and one-of-a-kind person, you present your own set of feelings. What is wrong with that? Okay, I am sitting here answering my own question. I am sure that many people think that I might need to tweak some of my feelings when they come out of my mouth the way they do! I work on that a lot.

Just for a minute, let's play the Dr. Patient game. I will write a word down (already been done), and then you say the first word you think of. For example, my word is *yellow*. Your word is *sun*.

1. angry _____
2. happy _____
3. family _____
4. red _____
5. dirty _____
6. friendly _____
7. green _____
8. thankful _____

You get the picture of how the game works. Your answers show what you are really thinking at the moment, and some of your true feelings might be revealed. I really like to do this because it helps me see where I'm at along my journey of self-evaluation.

If you are honest and say the first word that pops in your mind, you could see a pattern. Your pattern might help you see how many positive or negative traits or thoughts or feelings are moving through your head or heart. If the negative outweigh the positive, the work should begin.

We cannot have all positive 24-7—impossible. I mean we are actively participating in real life. Life really is a reality show! I am not that naïve, but if you tip the feelings scale with too much negativity, I am thinking you are not as happy as you can be!

When your feelings are low, exhausted, abused, or have been wronged, what do you do to recover? Are you resilient? What is resiliency? The definition states that it is rebounding, springing back, or regrouping. Have you been successful in attempting to rebound? I have to ask some hard questions.

It is so easy for all of us to try to stay in our comfort zones. We find our little niches, and we tend to want to stay there. You have heard that ole saying you can't teach an old dog new tricks. I am not an old dog; I am just an older dog. And I get it about learning new tricks! When I meet people who are very comfortable in their ruts or their very own niche, it can be very intimidating to try to convince anyone to move out. And to be asked to make some new changes for the better is like pulling teeth. It hurts and is really not what you want to do. It can be a shock to your system.

I think we all need to try to learn a little flexibility and resiliency, if needed. If a person is ever confronted with abuse; neglect; a failed marriage; violence; low self-esteem; the loss of a spouse, child, family member, friend, a pet; etc., one needs to know how to accept and adjust. More on these words later.

Tips

How about some pick-me-ups, mood-lifting tricks like two minutes to happiness?

Flip through old photos—ooh and ah—see how skinny you were in high school. Sorry, maybe you should skip this tip. Might depress you.

Munch on nuts: walnuts, really any nuts, or sneak salmon into your salad for lunch. Omega 3 wards off the big D.

Aromatherapy, a favorite of mine. Light a favorite candle or use a diffuser especially where open flame is a no-no. Might try lavender for calm. We could all use some calm!

Open your shades. Let the sunshine in! You know, science tells us that we all need fifteen minutes of sunshine each day!

Walk around the block. Combine numbers four and five. Go outside and walk. Studies show that people who get light exposure during the day sleep better and have less D'sion. (Depression—there, I spelled it out. Didn't want to though.) The light exposure also keeps you more alert and productive. And even light exercise like walking can lift your mood.

Clear the clutter. Straighten up your desk or shelf at home. You can make piles, but make them neat.

Think fast. Turn your thoughts into a race. It can lift the blues in a minute. Research shows that rapid thinking may release feel-good brain chemical, or it could just be a helpful distraction.

Cue up YouTube. A hearty laugh produces a chemical reaction that instantly elevates your mood, reduces pain and stress, and boosts immunity. When stress rises and you are fixing to blow, make yourself giggle!

Chop veggies. Enough said, just don't chop your fingers.

Do a good deed either for someone else or yourself. Who wins? Both!

Religion

At the very beginning of this adventure, I included religion as a possible chapter. You will notice that this chapter is very short in comparison to the others, not because of the importance or integrity of the subject but more of the facts or truth of the matter. I googled (you all know that word) a question: how many books, written and published, are there about religion?

Mr. or Miss Google answered back that that question was hard to answer, but they did give me an audit number of four days ago when I asked. Google says at that time of January 24, 2021, there were 178,221,216 books referencing religion in some way. My opinion—who am I to try to give another opinion on this topic as there are already 178 million books that have probably got religion covered!

There are roughly 4,200 religions, churches, groups, movements, faith groups, etc. I do believe that 99 percent of the people worldwide believe in a higher power. I do. Do you? I am in no way saying to you that you have to believe in God or your higher power, but with all of this seventy-six-year-old's experience, I am pretty sure that all of my bad stuff in my life would have been much *worser* if I had not been very up close and personal with my God.

One tip on religion, everyone on this planet earth has, is, or will go through *it* (bad stuff), some or a lot! I said everyone, some more than others.

Tip

    Drumroll, please.
    Do not try to go through *it* alone no matter how big or small. Your small could be my big, and vice versa. Share your scary, sad, lonely, desperate, doomed, D'ed, angry, anxious, beaten, belittled, bullied, broken, broken-up, battered, worrying, etc. thoughts and or actions. With whom? There will be a list near the end.

The Good, the Bad, and the Ugly

I am not sure that I understood the interpretations of the three topics in the movie, but I do like the title. Probably most of us have our own version of what is good, bad, and ugly in our lives. Think of any subject or topic, and there are gazillions (love to create new words!). And I believe we all take and use a different spin on it.

We all do tweak a lot, and I am trying to leave politics out of this entirely. Yes, I agree that all can say that between COVID and politics, 2020 was a very rough year. And now in 2021, I am trying even harder to find that light at the end of the tunnel.

I am positive there will a good, strong light! Wow, just talking about it, I'm already beginning to see the shining! Hope you can too. Many things that have happened in my life have led me to this conclusion: the best coping skill that we all have lies within us is our attitude. Like the little train trying to get up and over the big hill, "I think I can. I think I can." The train thought he/she could, and it did! I know every one of you have gotten over big and small hills that you never thought possible.

We do not want to dwell on the last two—the bad and the ugly. I know they have and are happening in your life, maybe daily. You may think it will never end. That is where your pessimism is lurking and is locked in and is understandable if you have had your run of bad luck.

I also recognize the fact that some people tend to attract bad luck! I am truly sorry if that is or has been happening to you. If you have been in a rut for some time, you may be very pessimistic, down on yourself, D'ed (remember, that stands for depressed—I just really don't like that word), or just plain tired of it all. Most people, I believe, are to be an optimist or a positive person.

Remember, when you were a little child, you didn't know any better then. You looked forward to getting up to play and have fun. What happened and when did it happen that you realized that it sometimes is an ugly world and no happy days are here again?

For most, the downward spiral is caused by a terrible event or another person's actions, right? Some of this ugly came from an outside force, some brought on by yourself. In either case, this is where one has to hunker down and dig deep within ourselves and remember that you really want to seek and find the good. This discussion tends to remind me of the Serenity Prayer (nonbelievers, please just listen to the words). Basically, TSP says to accept the things you cannot change, change the things you can change, and use your obtained wisdom to know the difference. I really have to work on that last part as I question my own wisdom.

Basically, the human being seeks good and happiness and peace. This may be much harder if you have been in a long-running pattern of bad and ugly. I have witnessed many people that have accomplished the change in their lives from bad/ugly to good. Was it easy? For most, a big fat *no*.

You must remember, the good and positive things in your life are worth fighting for! And I am not talking about literally fighting, like fighting-out-behind-the-barn fighting. You know what I mean. There is so much self-talk, reading, yoga, eating the right foods, supplements, exercise that says it will help us, mind and body. Try some of the above. Most of the time, if you believe that it will help, it probably will!

Are you your own worst enemy? Welcome to the club. Have you ever said, "I don't feel like doing that," or "I can't do that," or "I don't wanna try that. It's too scary"? There might be a lot to be said about if at first you don't succeed, try and try again. You know that saying. Just saying.

We would be remiss if we did not address crime, the law, and punishment. How old were you when you developed your conscience? I guess some are still looking. Was it when your mom caught you sneaking one more cookie from the cookie jar, knowing you had been told no more cookies 'til after dinner'?

I remember my mom or dad catching me in some little white lies. But catch me, they did! I remember at a very young age that I was to never steal or lie. I was not really sure why, but they both convinced me that there were and always would be consequences of doing bad. If I followed my parents' rules, there would be good. I would get enough cookies, and my parents would be happy and all is good.

Things just began to start to maybe make sense to try to do the right thing. Wrong actions meant consequences! For every action, there is a reaction. Is that physics? I loved science and still do, but physics was not my strongest course. I like more life science actually, but just teaching and learning good is much more productive for all.

Now I am not naïve enough to believe that everyone of us have, are, or will never do wrong or break the law. Yes, I had one or more speeding tickets—oops! None of those were in recent years but back in my younger days. I guess I grew up and realized I would rather spend my money on other things.

When we commit a wrong of any kind, today we try to correct it, change plans, or commit to not making the same mistake again. Change some bad habits, and you will feel so much better and maybe more peaceful, which is such a good feeling.

You will notice that I have used the word *good* many more times than the word *bad*. It is my belief that the more we all see the word *good* in print or we hear the word *good* often, it will become ingrained in our head. That is not a bad thing.

Also, I have tried to capitalize the word *good*—the more attention to the good than bad. We are trying to ingrain good into the brain. Guess I would rather focus on good, good, good. The bad is going to happen in spite of. The ugly is going to happen in spite of. We don't even have to think about it; it can just jump on us when we are totally unaware. So when it does, we need to *accept* it has happened, then adjust. Making that a habit will eventually turn your mental attitude more positive.

Tips

Accept the good. Accept the bad. Accept the ugly.
Adjust, adjust, adjust. All of the above.
Do not forget to do the deep breathing exercises in all of the above. Do the breathing exercise any time you think of it. The breathing routine reminds me of the song "I Feel Good." Listen to it, and you will feel good. Oh, James Brown did the song. Maybe a little shooby-do-be-do.

Teaching

Teach, verb: (1) to impact knowledge of or skill in; (2) give instruction.

Teachable, adjective: (1) capable of being instructed; (2) capable of being taught on a subject.

Teacher, noun: (1) one who teaches or instructs especially as a profession, instructor.

Teaching, noun: (1) act of one who or that which teaches; (2) that which is taught, a doctrine or precept.

I could not attempt to produce a book without including this chapter after having spent over half of my life dearly connected to the profession of teaching. It has been a trip or journey that I have really enjoyed. Oh yes, there have been a few hills or sometimes mountains to climb, but I think we got up and over in due time. There were some days that I am pretty sure I had to be that little choo choo train trying to get up the hill. "I think I can. I think I can." Most times, I thought I could, and I did!

I went to college for four years to get a degree to teach, and I have been in the teaching profession fifty-plus years. I believe this is the first time that I have ever looked up the definitions above. Teaching is an ever-evolving process. Even though I have had over fifty years of experience in the teaching profession, I still remain absolute that the day that I stop learning something new is the day I need to stop and regroup. Teaching and learning go hand in hand.

Of the four definitions about teaching, I believe the word *teachable* to be the most important. I also believe that everyone can teach something to others. On the other hand, I have met some that were not very teachable. I am not speaking of the intelligence level. I am speaking of attitude about learning.

In the early years of our marriage, my husband was not only a teacher, he was a coach in junior high school and later in high school. Many students or athletes are naturals in athletics. A sport or all sports just comes natural to them or is very easy for them. Some students really want it. They really want to learn the sport of football. They are very coachable or teachable.

And then, there is the other group, or students that were in athletics or PE just because they were made to be or they have to get the credit! My husband always loved the challenge and was usually up for it. He actually turned some of the uncoachables into very good athletes with good teaching and coaching skills.

He created a premier physical education program in a junior high school that got all the kids interested in PE. One unit in his program was learning how to swim, do archery, play ping-pong, and many other sports because Coach King tried some creative and new teaching skills with some kids who had not had the opportunity to even like learning and having fun while doing it.

There really are more ways to skin a rabbit! You can learn to learn and can have fun learning, and you can learn to be teachable. Coach King actually turned some of his uncoachables into very good athletes with his very good teaching and coaching skills. He still hears from some of his recruits.

The same traits and attitude apply in the classroom. Present the facts, truth, and subject matter in a way that all of the students can learn at their pace and have fun at the same time. Who wins? The students, teachers, parents, administrators, support staff—well, everybody connected to the school setting. It's a win-win deal!

He and I have found that patience and perseverance definitely are virtues in the teaching, coaching, and parenting professions. We are both so glad that we had a few years in teaching or coaching before we had our children because we learned a lot from teaching and coaching that we applied to our parenting library.

We have a daughter-in-law who is a teacher and a son-in-law who is an administrator in the education field. Our hats are off to them for doing a great job before and during the Covid crisis. Thank you!

We have another daughter-in-law who is tenacious, perseverant, and successful in a helping field in business. Our daughter is a nurse practitioner in her practice. Our two sons are primarily in the business world, and we have witnessed all in teaching and teachable moments.

And, thank goodness, all of the abovementioned family are very involved in teaching, teaching, teaching our six grands every day and night. As most everyone knows, that is the most important teaching job in the world. (Not too sure who is teaching or learning the most?) Rex and I want to thank all six adults publicly for who they are and for the beautiful gift of our six grands. You have and/or are hitting a grand slam or outta the ballpark every day!

Now, has every one of the six adults' lives or days been a walk in the park every day? They will be the first to tell you no! They can all remember the very worst day of their lives, and in the next memory photo remember, but we got through it. They learned from the worst day and have been able to teach about it the next bad day.

Teaching and learning, learning and teaching, it all goes hand in hand. Funny how it works that way. You say, "Well, I didn't like how that ended." Okay, maybe you didn't like it, but maybe you learned something from it—also known as accept and adjust!

Tips

Try to gain the serenity to accept the things you cannot change. Try to gain the courage to change the things you can. And definitely try to gain the wisdom to know the difference!

The three tips above sound a lot like choices. Make good ones.

My wish for each of you is to try to learn one new thing each day. Be teachable! Not only will you be wiser, but you will be a happier camper.

Aging

The word *age* can be a very volatile topic. Have you ever been in the company of several women? One of these women is the most beautiful and poised and graceful woman in the room until a clueless person asks Mrs. All-Put-Together her age. Wow! Ole Clueless is really naïve or very stupid. A suggestion for Clueless is to do your research on the person you are quizzing about age to see if you dare go there.

I guess I personally am the total opposite. As I have been up close and personal several times to the Pearly Gates, I am more than happy to reveal my age. I am thrilled to gain another birthday. It is all in one's perspective!

Not long ago, I was with a family that had a three-year-old, and this lady says, "Hi, baby girl" to the little girl.

The baby girl screams back, "I am not a baby. I am a big girl!" And yet another perspective about age.

And then there is the sixteen-year-old who looks like he is twenty-two and walks into the liquor store to buy a six-pack. There is an undercover officer in the store. I guess age does make a difference to some folks.

As I mentioned my close trip to the Pearly Gates, I definitely have a different perspective on age and aging. At age forty-six, I entered the year 1991 with a life-threatening event. Obviously, I made it, but I can tell you that I want people to ask my age.

I love celebrating every birthday. I guess I am very happy to be alive. Things looked very bleak for about a year. The year of 2006 brought another big event for the King family. I was diagnosed with colon cancer. Made it again! I can't leave out the year 2013 (not sure if thirteen is my lucky number), as I had a heart attack. I don't think many of my family members appreciated my statement I made as they were rolling me out of the cath lab with two stents. "I didn't croak!" I only wanted to break the ice for them. They all looked so solemn.

After these three big events, gratitude and a very positive attitude has become my mantra. I am pretty sure the first event helped me with the following second and third events. I know I became much stronger physically and mentally. Well, definitely, it was all a mental game changer. Plus, I had much help and wonderful support from my family, friends, and our church family.

I could have never gained as I did alone. So I did keep aging from forty-six to the ripe ole age of seventy-six, but you know I was already aging from birth or conception to now, every minute of every day. And no, I will not get into the when-does-life-begin thingy. I *do* know when my life began, and I am and will continue to be eternally grateful!

Let's just say, from the beginning, you and me—all of us—are unique! There is only one of you. You have one body and one mind. Please take care of it. It's not so much as what happens to us every day, but how we take care of ourselves and what we do with our unique self!

Our own self is our responsibility. We very seldom get do-overs or a chance to redo good or bad events in life. How good would it be if everybody would learn from their own mistakes, not make that same one again, and make better choices the next time? Utopia?

Our living or our life is pretty much a journey moving from day one to last day. Explore all of your milestones that you have accomplished and enjoy every pleasant memory of the past. Do not stop there; continue to make new ones every day. Life is never over 'til it's over! Remember all of your happy times and create new ones. Keep doing this daily because you can be a happy person.

You will enjoy the aging process more if you genuinely seize your moment, even the simple ones. Actually, I believe you might enjoy the simple pleasures more than the complicated ones. Complicated ones involve much more work on your part and sometimes much more worrying. Ever caught yourself worrying about having really nothing to worry about? Keep reading!

Almost always, too much worrying will cause you much frustration. Think of all the moments that you have spent worrying about that_____. You may have sulked, cried, screamed, wrung your hands, and added more wrinkles to your already lined beautiful face. And did all of the above solve or even help your situation? I'm guessing a big fat *no*. Were you exhausted after the above scene? I'm guessing a big fat *yes*.

I cannot speak enough about the great side effects of seeking and finding the simple pleasures of life. If you have not started to seek simple pleasures yet, make a vow today to at least start with one hide-and-go-seek pleasure today. If you are discombobulated today, you have already hidden some of your pleasures.

You are ready to now seek some good stuff waiting for you. I do believe *all* of us have some good or, at least, better stuff (pleasures) waiting for us out there. I make no promises, just suggestions or tips to help you get started. You do realize that some of the very best good stuff or pleasures are usually right under your nose: family, kids, playing in the park, going for a walk, taking time to smell the roses, watching the sun set, etc.

You are sitting there thinking, *I am sixty-one years old. And my life is dull, boring, or just plain ole ugly. I am never happy, never have been, and I don't see it getting any better at this age.* You do know, in most cases like yours, you do have a choice to continue down that miserable road or path, or you can start with one small change physically or mentally or both. Remember, we really cannot separate our physical from our mental state. They are totally connected.

If you attempt to make good or better choices daily, you will get better at choice making. It might even become a good habit. Good habits are hard to break. Do *not* say bad habits are hard to break!

Kids of *all* ages, let this become your daily mantra: try to always do the right thing. Most people, I truly believe, basically know right from wrong. Yes, we sometimes go off the rail, but hopefully, you can rein yourself back on the good track. Kids and teens, this is hard, but the sooner you figure this out, the better life will treat you (and parents too). You have to keep working hard, and eventually, it will work for you. It's hard for adults too. I just derailed recently!

All of this last paragraph is essentially called aging or maturing. Note, kids and teens, I have known many adults and seniors that are still seeking a good aging or maturing process. So see, there's always hope that things will get better or simple AND easier! My advice to all: don't ever, ever give up. Aging or maturing, I'm admitting, can be a booger bear sometimes; but I assure you (no promises but close), it—whatever *it* is, maybe life—is very, very much worth it!

At seventy-six, I would not trade my 27,740 plus days. What about those near-death days, you ask? I am so sorry that my family had to go through that, but we all did survive it and maybe for the better, mentally. Physically, I'm not so sure, but I am still kicking, just not very high. I honestly do not want to repeat those bad days. But what I can say about those days is they really made me stronger and more determined to live every day I have left to the fullest, laugh more—all those lines on my face you thought were aging lines? Oh no, they are laughter lines—smile more, and love, love, love. I am so ever thankful. I try to count my blessings every day instead of complaining about what I don't have.

Get positive and stay positive!—quote from Sharla King, LPC, wife, mother, and meme. (Disclaimer: I do not guarantee results for you. I just know most of my tips have worked for me. They are simply suggestions for you, but I do double dare you to try some or all of them!)

Tips

Just reread this chapter. Aging is a good gig, just stay with *it* 'til it's your time.

Laugh, laugh, laugh (within boundaries).

What I Have Learned

During my aging process, I think I have learned a lot. I had good teachers in school (Sunday school—I got lots of blue stars on the chart). The Sunday teachers only had to put up with me one day a week, and my poor public school teachers had me all five days of the week. And I usually had perfect attendance.

I might have been one of those kids that the teachers wished would take a day off occasionally. It was not going to happen as I loved school. The best aromatherapy for me was opening that brand-new box of crayons that my parents bought for me at the beginning of every school year in elementary. It always meant a new adventure with my friends. Nostalgia, nothing like it. I also had some very good mentors in my family and friends.

I usually made good grades; but I was the kid that memorized the material right before the test, hopefully passed the test, and then moved on to the next lesson. Retaining all of that information was usually hard and continues to be a problem today.

I feel sure we really all do have very different learning styles. I did not like pop tests. But guess who, as a teacher, gave pop tests to her students? Go figure. Do unto others as you would have them do unto you, biblically speaking. Guess I was, am, and always will be a teacher at heart.

Would like to share a few "I Have Learned" quotes from K. G. Bush's *Hidden Strengths*. There are several. I do not expect you to delve into each and think each is profound; but I find almost all of them are so good, honest, and yes, profound.

I have learned that you cannot make someone love you. All you can do is be someone who can be loved. The rest is up to them. (A gone-wrong marriage or relationship?)

It takes years to build up trust and only seconds to destroy it.

It's not what you have in your life but who you have in your life that counts.

You can do something in an instant that will give you heartache for life.

No matter how thin you slice it, there are always two sides.

It's taken me a long time to be the person I want to be.

Either you control your attitude, or it will control you.

Learning to forgive takes practice.

Money is a lousy way of keeping score.

Sometimes when I am angry, I have the right to be angry, but that doesn't give me the right to be cruel.

Just because someone doesn't love you the way you want them to doesn't mean they don't love you with all they have.

No matter how good a friend is, they're going to hurt you every once in a while, and you must forgive them.

Our background and our circumstances may have influenced who we are, but we are responsible for who we become.

Sometimes when my friends fight, I'm forced to choose sides even when I don't want to.

Just because two people argue, it doesn't mean they don't love each other. And just because they don't argue doesn't mean they do.

Two people can look at the exact same thing and see something totally different.

No matter how you try to protect your children, they will eventually get hurt, and you will hurt in the process.

Your life can be changed in a matter of hours by people who don't even know you.

The people you care most about in life can be taken from you too soon.

It's hard to determine where to draw the line between being nice and not hurting people's feelings and standing up for what you believe.

Your life counts, and it's up to you to make sure it counts. This life is not a rehearsal, so make the most of it.

Take total self-care. This body is for life, the only one you will have.

Always be optimistic and adopt a positive attitude. Things are never as bad as they seem.

Learn to forgive and let go. This is the key for making all relationships loving.

Be childlike in your approach to life. Live with joy. Laugh a lot. Be lighthearted and happy.

No matter how much I care, some people just don't care back.

You can get by on charm for about fifteen minutes. After that, you had better know something.

You should always leave loved ones with loving words. It may be the last time you see them.

Regardless how hot and steamy a relationship is at first, the passion fades and there had better be something else to take its place.

No matter how bad your heart is broken, the world doesn't stop for your grief.

There are many ways of falling and staying in love.

Always have integrity with yourself and others. Do what you say you will, and own up when you don't.

Live with an attitude of gratitude to bring so much goodness back into your life. We live in a truly abundant world. There is more than enough for all of us.

People are so amazing and never cease to surprise with their capacity of goodness. Always give them the benefit of the doubt and know that they are doing the best that they can.

There is so much beauty all around us, it takes our breath away. You just have to see things through new eyes.

Tips

Only one—take life in and breathe deep!

Positives to Consider

I am a unique and precious human being, always doing the best that I can and growing in wisdom and love. I am one of a kind. That's right; there's only one of me in the world.

I am in charge of my own life.

My first responsibility is to my own growth and well-being. The better I am to me, the better I will be to others.

I will become responsible for my own decisions and assume responsibility of the outcome of these decisions. I will use all outcomes in a positive and constructive manner.

I will actively participate in my life.

I am gentle and forgiving toward myself and capable of freeing myself of animosity or resentment.

I am who I am, and I love and accept myself totally and unconditionally. Love yourself, then you can love others better.

I have the right and the responsibility to ask for help when I am feeling stuck in my emotions, behavior, and attitude.

I am never alone. I am filled with and walk in love and light. I simply need to slow down enough to experience the power within me.

Tip

Only one. Without a doubt, I know that if you stay straight today and do the best that you can, good things will happen to you in spite of yourself.

Rules for Being Human

I have never been big on lots of rules, but almost from the day we are born, it seems to be that we are subjected to rules.

When you were born, you did not come with an owner's manual. I wanted a methodical, exact manual. You know, ABC, 1-2-3 list to take home with me when I left the hospital with twin boys in 1975. I did not receive such a list. I found out really quick that it was (1) feed, (2) burp, (3) change diaper, (4) get them to sleep, and hang on!

I still believe guidelines make life work better. I had to develop my own with those baby boys! Nine years later, when our daughter was born, I had forgotten all of the parenting skills I had learned; so I had to start over. She was a girl. New skills were required.

You will receive a body and a mind. You may like it or dislike it, but it is the only thing you are sure to keep for the rest of your life.

You will learn lessons in the informal school of Life University. Every person in the world is enrolled. (And you don't like competition?)

There are no mistakes, only lessons. Growth is a process of experimentation. Failures are as important as success. Think how much you learned from your failures! I should be one smart cookie by now! I am not sure how our three children grew up as sane as they are with all of my mistakes!

Our twins were two weeks old. We were home, and Grandmother was still there helping out (thank goodness). It was time to start their vitamins. Back then, they were that thick molasses-looking goop in a bottle. Grandmother was holding one, Rex the other. I instructed them to open each baby's mouth so I could squirt a dropper full of molasses into those rosebud mouths. I did, and would you believe they both stopped breathing at the same time?

So the three adults in the room panicked for a second, and finally, someone thought to do CPR on a very small scale for babies. And both babies at the same time let out a blood-curdling cry. Thank goodness! We were all crying then, but our boys were breathing once again.

The next morning ding-a-ling to the pediatrician, how do I give the vitamins? Simple, you mix them in their formula once a day. "Oh yes. Well, thank you, doctor." Goodbye until tomorrow's call. Pretty sure we put the doctor's phone number in our speed dial list. I'm pretty sure neither one of our sons take vitamins to this day. I think they're both pretty healthy.

You will know when you have learned a lesson when your actions change. Wisdom is practice. A little of something is better than a lot of nothing.

Your life is up to you. Life provides the canvas; you do the painting. Take charge of your life, or someone else will.

Tip

Try to follow the rules!

My Absolutely—My Very Last Tip List And You Really Must Do These!

Mental or emotional health refers to your overall psychological well-being. It includes the way you feel about yourself, the quality of your relationships, and your ability to manage your feelings and deal with difficulties.

Strong, mentally healthy people, move on. No big pity parties. Embrace change. Stay happy. They are kind, fair, unafraid to speak up, and willing to take calculated risks. Celebrate others success with no resentment.

Is your life on autopilot, just going through the motions day after day? Then one day you wake up and you find yourself older (remember, not old, just *-er*) and realize you haven't really lived life? Any regrets?

Okay, by now you have read most of my tips at the end of each chapter. The following is a general list of reminders to sum up our tips. If you can and want to, take one, use it, make it your own like a habit; and you will be on your way to a happier, healthier lifestyle. And, do not forget, after you have conquered one good tip or habit, continue to add another one or two. Do not forget to add some physical ones too because we absolutely cannot separate your mental health from your physical health or body. It's like peas and carrots, glued at the hip, etc. You get the picture. All the above is one—you!

Enjoy and pick your faves.

Improve your physical health and automatically experience greater mental and emotional health by getting enough sleep and rest. Most people need seven to eight hours of sleep each night.

Learn and practice good nutrition. Eat those peas and carrots! They really are good for you. Don't like 'em? Choose other veggies!

Exercise to relieve stress and lift your mood. To get the most mental health benefits, shoot for thirty minutes or more each day. Move it or lose it. Move it or lose it!

Get a good dose of sunshine every day. Try to get, at least, fifteen minutes of sun every day. If you can't go outside, stand by a window and dream of spring.

Limit alcohol and avoid cigarettes and other bad drugs. (I was so happy last week, one of my doctors ceased one of my drugs.) The abovementioned things might give you a good buzz or high temporarily, and then you wake up, with not near as much fun.

Improve your mental skills. Do things that positively impact others. Practice self-discipline.

As mentioned earlier, make it a goal to learn one new thing every day. Let's call it intellectual candy. Take a class, join a book club, volunteer, travel, etc. When my kids were bored and didn't have anything to do, I always said I would take them to the library, and they could spend their summer afternoon reading at the library. They weren't fans of my idea, so they got unbored. Even meditation is doing something good mentally!

While getting your fifteen minutes of sunshine, enjoy all the nature around you. Just walking through a garden can lower your blood pressure and reduce stress.

Get a pet. If that's impossible, go to a pet store or zoo and watch and enjoy animals.

Make leisure time a priority. Do things for no other reason than it just feels good to do them. Read a good book, a real book like this one in your hand. Okay, I will allow some online stuff. Listen to music. Light a candle while taking a bubble bath—yummy! When was your last bubble bath? Even you guys?

These tips are combo (sounds like we have skipped out to McDonalds) tips, both physical and mental. Some overlap; but if they are that good, they are worth repeating, right?

Love anything and everything. Remember, it does not have to be romantic love, even though I am not opposed to it. My husband and I celebrate fifty-three years this year.

Get outside. Do not hole up inside or indoors! Go out and walk in the rain. I love the song "Singing in the Rain." If you just cannot get outside, open the shades and/or windows.

Savor food. Do not just eat for the sake of eating or because it is twelve o'clock at noon. Really enjoy it. I do believe the cooking shows on TV have helped us learn to enjoy our food much better.

Get out of your cubicle or rut. I have heard many say that one positive from the COVID virus is that it has allowed people to work from home. May be positive or negative? Another way to look at it is look at all that bonding with the family!

Turn off your phone and TV! I have never seen so many literally glued to and some addicted to their phones. My kids fuss at me and say that my phone is never on; not true. I never turn it off. I just do not carry it with me!

Travel. Do not forget that if a long, expensive vacation trip is not in your game plan, there are some exciting places, usually local, that you have never been to or not seen. Try them.

Rediscover. What is really important to you? Some might call this your bucket list.

Eliminate the stuff, things that literally waste your time. And don't sweat the small stuff, for it's all small stuff.

Exercise. I said some overlap, but this one is worth repeating. Can't say enough. Move it or lose it!

Be positive. I am sure by now you have noticed that I have capitalized a few words here and there. I want you to see how important those words or concepts are to me. Positive gets you everywhere. Negative thoughts take you down. They do you or me *no* good. Right now, replace all negative with positive. You will feel so much better!

Kiss in the rain. With your mask on, of course! Just kidding. Just show your vaccination card. Seriously, try kissin' in the rain. It might make your head swim, then you'll feel better. Carpe diem—seize the moment!

Face your fears. I still cannot look a snake in the eye. I guess I need to work on that fear. But if you can, face up to the music and try to overcome whatever fear you might have or whatever you are afraid of and then be free of that fear.

When you suffer, suffer. Life is not all happy, happy. We all have sadness, sorrow, and suffering in our lives. We feel the pain. We lose loved ones, pets, jobs, homes. It is a part of life. Grieve, feel the pain. And when over it is over, move on, remember, and then find joy.

Slow down. We all are in too big of a hurry. It is not healthy—from eating, walking, driving, reading, etc. Take time and enjoy what you do. But do take time to smell the roses.

Volunteer. Help at school, work with children and your neighbors (do you know their names?) and civic groups, etc.

Talk to older people. We really are interesting sometimes. Most are wise, experienced, and would enjoy talking and visiting with you. They or we can tell good stories, maybe even some whoppers.

Do nothing. I know, I know. Nearly every page of this book with the tips, we are advocating and sharing thoughts of *doing* this or that. Now, I am saying do nothing. For many, this is one of the hardest: learning to be still, silent, to hear our inner voice, to be in tune with life. Do this daily.

Watch sunsets daily. One of the most beautiful times of the day is sunset. Most artists still strive to capture those beautiful colors on canvas.

Break out from those ruts. If you are in one, break out of it. Change things up. Look at things from a new perspective.

Stop watching the news. Enough said.

Cry, especially men. I have always been concerned about the boys in junior and high school and all of those pent-up emotions. I remember giving permission to several boys to cry. They did, and they felt better. No one saw them but me. Now, boys, girls, men, and women, do not make this a daily habit. I prefer that you laugh more than you cry, which brings me to my very last but probably the most important tip.

Laughter, laughter, laughter—the best medicine, and let me tell you why.

Laughter improves breathing. It clears mucus from the lungs, allowing them to expand and take in more oxygen.

Laughter reduces blood pressure by improving circulation and shooting oxygen and nutrients to tissues throughout the body.

Laughter heightens mental functions by increasing delivery of oxygen and produces a hormone to improve alertness and memory.

Laughter helps relieve pain by increasing delivery of oxygen and through the level of endorphins. The pain-killing chemicals are produced by the brain.

Now that you know that laughter is one of the healthiest things you can do for yourself, I am asking every one of you to give me a good ole belly laugh. Ah, come on, you can do better than that. I mean let it come from your toes all the way through your belly, up and out! Now, don't you feel better? I knew you would. Practice this exercise several times a day.

Another disclaimer. Some people laugh inappropriately. Please do not do that kind of laughter. If you do laugh inappropriately, you might need to make an appointment with a professional.

So now that you have laughed 'til you are crying and you are feeling *so* good, slow it down and let's do some deep breathing. Take a deep breath to the count of four through your nostrils. Exhale slowly through your mouth to the count of four.

Repeat three times. Now you should really feel good, kinda like melted butter flowing all over you. You are almost a puddle. Oh, you aren't feeling it? Practice, practice. But wait, I want you to finish the rest. You have got to read the good ole new and old quotes and summary.

Tips for the tips

Reread all twenty-two tips.

All of these tips are free. Yes, I said free. Number six might cost a little something if you leave your hometown, but you can even tweak that one according to your own pocketbook. Look at it this way. You could travel to your backyard to bird-watch or smell the roses. Still free stuff, right?

Good New and Old quotes That Are Actually True and Really Usable—or Isms

I love this word.
    I was, I am, and I will be positive.
    Don't sweat the small stuff. It's all small stuff.
Wherever you go, there you are!
"Accept and adjust," said my friend Richard.
Me, me, me does not work.
Sometimes, it really is all about me. (Just go with it; different situations.)
Fake it 'til you make it. Just never be 100 percent fake.
Carpe Diem—seize the moment.
You gotta be a friend to have a friend.
It's okay to not be okay.
Today is a good day to have a good day.
There is usually a light at the end of the tunnel.
There is always a reason to dance.
Be all that you can be…in the Army. I have been known to sing this jingle to my kids at school, my own kids, and now my senior kids. It makes for a good career/vocational tool. Yes, I rarely had any take me up on the military route, but it sometimes gave a totally blank career-minded kid an option to think about. "What do you want to be when you grow up?" That question was usually in most conversations even if they were there to talk about their girl or boyfriend. Always had to maneuver them to start planning.
This is the first day of the rest of your life.

Try to always do the *right* thing. Listen to your heart, brain, and grit (stop with that fifth cookie).

I think I can, I think I can, I think I can—little train going uphill.

Kenny Rogers tells us, "You've got to know when to hold 'em and know when to fold 'em."

He who laughs, lasts!

I feel better after I *wine* a little.

I saved the best for last.

"Don't should on yourself." Just let this one slowly sink in; i.e., just go ahead and do it. Don't waste time worrying about it. Like it? Thought so.

Tip

Just one. If you find just one or more of these isms or sayings funny or useful, please laugh out loud. Maybe even a belly laugh. You will feel so good!

The Short List

I have been trying to wind this book down a few chapters ago, but ideas just kept popping up. It really is not that I think I have all the answers to helping you find your good happy place or your happy middle or good mental health state. I just really feel so strongly about the status of our mental health in every person. I feel this way even though I know that we cannot have a utopic feel-really-good-and-happy world full of people.

I am hopefully about to finish this writing at the tail end of the pandemic or the COVID crisis. I feel so fortunate that my husband and I never got the COVID. We have gotten our second vaccination, and we are still praying for all of our family and friends and people all over the world to get and stay healthy physically and mentally. We have family members and friends who did get the virus and survived and are doing fine now. We continue to pray for those who lost family and friends.

Recently in the news, they reported that many of our teenagers' mental health is in great decline in the United States. Depression in our teens has risen to 97 percent, and the worst statistic of all, teen suicide has risen above 50 percent. Folks, these people are our kids!

America should never lose one child or teen to suicide or any mental health problem! And while here, the same goes for any "kid," zero to one hundred years old. Our veterans—many of whom are homeless—and many people of every kind, rank, and file are fighting for their lives with this monster disease. I have to be careful; I just might get on my mental health soapbox for all kids. I just may have been called Mama Bear with all my cubs of all ages.

Babies, children, teens, young adults, kids of all ages, zero to one hundred plus, are not expendable! We must help protect and give every person a reason to seek happiness and to live every day to the fullest of a long healthy life!

Okay, I am stepping down off that tall soapbox. And now here is the short list of the must dos toward getting and maintaining a happy life.

I feel an urgency to get this message to all.

Laugh 'til you cry sometimes, and love.

Take three good, deep breaths. Inhale slowly; exhale slowly.

Enjoy fifteen minutes of sunshine daily.

Smile if you cannot muster up a laugh.

Think, meditate to self.

Exercise: walk the dog, do chores or yard work, work out while watching TV, stand up and stretch, etc. Move it or lose it!

Find your positive.

Eat healthy: fruits, veggies, beans, fish, chicken, beef, etc. (A little Blue Bell never hurt anybody—calcium?). I have also been known to do a Cheetos–Dr. Pepper lunch—yummy. Just don't do it daily!

Sleep. Get enough of it if you can. Seven to eight hours is recommended.

Remember, you are unique and valuable! There is no one like you, so stick around.

No tips!

I just gave you the best ten!

Summary

You own one unique body, only one. Take good care of it. Do not abuse it in any way, mentally or physically.

You say, *Wait a minute. The mental area encompasses the body, head to toe.* We know this physical area does cover head to toe. Why did I cover the whole body with the mental tag? Please remember, one cannot separate the two; that is, our whole body, both physical and mental. If you get physically sick, it stretches you mentally. If you get down, depressed, or even worse, it makes you feel physically sick also. Either way, you cannot fix one without the other. I truly believe my 1991 "dying year" prepared me for my 2006 cancer event and my 2013 heart attack event. The strength that I gained mentally after 1991 paved a smoother road for my 2006 and 2013 battles.

When I realized that I was actually going to live in 1991, I became a very positive person. Positivity absolutely impacted the physical diseases I would later endure. My family were and are so very thankful and grateful. One has a smoother life in transition sharing some thankfulness and gratitude. I cannot say that every day since has just been looking through rose-colored glasses or every day is not problematic.

On the contrary, ole Arthur*itis* comes to call regularly, and a few pains here and there. But are there many out there that are not experiencing the same? I still have issues, problems, or things that just don't go my way, but who says my way is the best way as I try to convince my husband? The difference now and when I was forty-six years old is I stop, think, rethink, and act slowly.

I will admit that my family and friends, and doctors, really know quite a bit more than I know about some other stuff! And as my older friend Richard says, his life message—and now mine too—is accept and adjust. Think about this; kinda says it all. These three words are really hard concepts for some; but if you are trying to reach a goal of peacefulness, happiness, contentment, and more in your life, then make it easier on yourself. If you let it be, it can be simple.

Please do not get derailed and start bringing up all of your buts—but I can't, but I don't want to, but…

You would be spinning your wheels and maybe even digging that deep, dark hole or well even deeper. Get on the positive train!

I do not promise you a rose garden or even that you will not get derailed a few times, but please find your way back on to the train and let's roll, as Todd said on the plane going toward the Pentagon that fateful day in 2001. Sometimes, it really is mind over matter.

I truly have written this book with my heart, mind, body, and soul. I have tried to give you a glimpse of my and my family's life and a few adversities; but looking back, I am sure there have been many more blessings. I am positive there have been many more laughs and smiles than crying jags. I sincerely hope I didn't bore you too badly by showing you some of my scars!

I know many of you have many scars from the past and probably more than enough current ones. Now don't go looking for any new ones! I have also learned that when I might be coming up with a good ole pity party for myself, I pause and think to try to look around. And usually, I find something positive right under my nose. There is always someone a lot worse off than me! So I try to snuff it up, get my big-girl panties on, and move on. And remember Richard's quote, "Accept and adjust!"

Do I believe in my free tips, exercises, and the statements that I have made? Absolutely, I do. And bet your booty I do! Do I do all of them all the time? No, no, no. Sometimes, I do not practice what I preach! If a few worked some of the time, what would happen if you tried more all of the time? We all might become Superman/Superwoman or Popeye with all of that energy. He is the reason I serve sautéed spinach weekly!

No book would be complete without a recipe. Every person in the world eats something, so we all love to share recipes. Here's mine. Use a large skillet, add some olive oil, dump in some chopped garlic, heat for a minute or two—don't overcook. Add a package of fresh spinach, and sprinkle with salt and black pepper to your taste. When the spinach has wilted, serve. Voila! Hope you enjoy. I now feel better that I have included at least one recipe, and it's a healthy one.

Back to task at hand, yes, I have tried all of my tips and suggestions. For me, some worked better than others. Remember, we are all different and unique. I would implore each of you, young and older and in between (age-wise), to start small. Choose one chapter or topic that you are most interested in. Try one or two of the tips, practice them, give it a try, and see if you see any improvement in whatever you are going through. I might not expect you teens to go to the topic on aging first even though every day in reality, you are aging. Who knows, you might get a kick out of our older thoughts!

Speaking of teenagers, I guess I agonize more over your teenage days than some others. I had the privilege of being a school counselor in elementary, junior high, and high school. I was in high school for twenty years, plus I had a captive audience. That doesn't mean that you had to listen to me. You were just exposed to maybe a different perspective. I always tried to remember that you were "too young for that and too old for that." Kinda puts you in a bind, huh?

All of your problems at that moment were very big to you. I never tried to fix your problems, maybe just offer some solutions and then let you choose which way to go. You usually chose the right way and came out better for making the right choice. You stopped, came and asked for some help, thought, rethought, and then acted. Amazing how that usually works.

My hat is off to you teenagers. No wonder you stay confused and unsure of yourself and the world around you. You are exposed to so much negativity and bad and ugly things. I urge you to not watch the news. I am trying to ween off of it. Just give me the weather. Get some good information from your parents.

While still at home in high school, I sometimes thought that my parents were really kinda dumb or stupid. There, I said it, admitted it. When I graduated and left home to go to college, my parents became the smartest parents in the world. I gained an instant new perspective! Good info can come from other family, friends, and people you know and trust.

Hang in and hold on. Most of this too will pass. The sun will come up tomorrow, and you will have a brand-new day and chance to accept and adjust!

If any of you reading this book are my former students, remember that I still love you and care about you, even you ornery ones! Would love to hear from you. I usually asked you what you wanted to be when you grew up. It seems I had very limited time with you. Those dedicated teachers felt that they really needed to teach you your ABCs and writin' and arithmetic, and they were mostly successful with a lot of hard work!

I highly respect the field of education and educators. Everyone needs and deserves an education. In all of my thirty-nine years in education, these are some of my thoughts. I was Ole Mother Hubbard living in my shoe. I gathered all of my schoolchildren in my shoe and protected them and educated them, and nobody better not even think about messing with them! Each child or teenager deserves a good, strong, and happy education! Who can argue with that?

Everyone suffers losses: death of a loved one, loss of a one-time opportunity, a job, a pet, or the trauma of a severe disappointment. There is more to you and your life than what you are now suffering. If you can harness in the pain of your body, mind, and spirit, you will kick-start a creative process that will nurture the healing of your whole self.

If you have battled depression, anxiety, stress, or worse for a long period of time, please seek help immediately from someone you trust in the mental health field. You might start with your family doctor and, if needed, he/she could refer you to a mental health professional.

Please, oh please, always keep a goal going in your life to find and keep yourself in your happy place. I'm not saying that we can all stay happy 24-7. But we all should want to seek a life of contentment, peace, happiness, and gratefulness because we know that life is going to throw us some curve balls, throw up some big and small hurdles, and maybe throw us under the bus.

We can always expect some downright bad stuff. We can't stay in a state of pessimism. We have to seek our middle zone. Enjoy the party times, flowers, balloons, and candy. We have to prepare for the D times, the bad, and the ugly. Coping skills readily come in handy. We have to get ready to meet those days that threaten our good, happy days!

Hopefully, this book has given you some convenient, cheap, useful tips on how to keep from falling into the deep, dark well we all fall in sometimes, and how to pull yourself up and out if you do fall in!

Get up and out and stay positive!

I have to believe that every living human being in the world (have gone universal) share the very same goal—to be happy in some shape or form. We all want and need to find our happy place. Even the naysayers, you and we are all vulnerable. So come on, boys and girls of all ages, seek, explore, and find your happy!

And I also believe that everybody needs a hug. So here is a hug from me to you. You should all enjoy this hug because this one is fat-free, sugar-free, requires no batteries, and relieves pain and depression (oops, I spelled it out).

We are all having a group hug. Feel it?

I can honestly say that is the biggest group hug I have ever had! Thank all you for participating.

Sources

There is a plethora (love this word) of mental health information. If there was not enough information prior to COVID-19 virus, check it out now. But the interesting thing I have discovered mostly on TV is the fact that reporters and journalists mention the fact that the COVID virus has exploited mental health, especially in our teenagers.

They say parents should be aware that there *could be* some long-term side effects for our children and teenagers. Seriously, Sherlock, you think? I am assuming that all school-age kiddos got up each morning, went to the breakfast table, and asked for the day's plan of schooling either from Alexa, their home computer, or parents if they had gotten the word.

The junior in high school might get to go to football practice and then rush over to the band hall, get in their pod to play their horn for thirty minutes, then go home, get on their computer, and do their math and reading assignments. The big brother has to babysit his younger sister also because it wasn't her day to go to first grade and mom had to go to work. Mom comes home at noon so Dad can go to work that afternoon. The next day, yesterdays' schedule was all changed again! Y'all, we might have some side-effect issues with our kids?

I am in no way blaming school officials for all of the eclectic decisions that have been made for the last year or so. Who did really know what to do or what was the right thing to do? It has kinda been who's-on-first mentality. Does the right hand know what the left hand is doing? Bottom line for me is that our kids have had to take it on the chin. We owe it to them to try to put Humpty Dumpty back together again! (I hope HD does not get canceled too!)

I saw a 97% increase in mental health problems for teenagers posted on TV. And even worse, we have a substantial increase in teenage suicides this past year. The majority of the parents of the teens who committed suicide that spoke on this topic said that their child took their life because of depression and not being allowed to attend school. We cannot and should not minimize this topic. I am all about *prevention* if at all possible. All of the chapters of this book tie into helping to prevent any kind of mental health illness.

Most of the written word is garnered from my many experiences of daily living and counseling situations. So thank you to all of the people who have crossed my path or I have crossed paths with. I did much reading, observing, and interacting with many people of all ages, again from zero to one hundred plus.

The media outlets included, but not limited to, ABC, CBS, CNN, Fox News, MSNBC, NBC, *New York Post*, endless websites, media outlets, forums, family, and friends.

After all that was involved into putting this book together, I attempted to fall back and heavily rely on common sense, and I sometimes wonder if common sense is a lost art!

I would like to give a big shout-out and thank you to our men and women serving, currently and previously, in our armed services in the USA and around the world, and to those who have fallen. We owe you all for the freedoms we so enjoy and for so much more.

Also, our first responders: doctors, nurses, policemen and policewomen, firefighters, and anyone serving in a helping field. Thank you! You are all so appreciated, and to all those who have died and their families. I also respect and admire the families of all the above. The above groups of people could not do the wonderful jobs they do without good support from families and friends. Another big thank you!

Credits

Mental Health America, Alexandria, Virginia
Positive Relationships, Counselingassociateshome.com, September, 14, 2011
American Psychiatric Association, Diagnostic & Statistical Manual of Mental Disorders, 5th Edition, DSM-5, Arlington, Virginia, 2013
Dr. Kathleen Light of University of North Carolina at Chapel Hill
Ohio State University–A study done on married couples on physical injuries...all I had.
Margarita Tartakovsky, MS Associated Editor at PsychCentral, August 4, 2019
Laurie Wilhelm–Express Yourself to Success.com
My friend Richard
Sarah Cain Spannagel, PhD, at Case Cam Western Reserve University, Family Circle, June 20, 2019
Ron Lieber, *The New York Times*
Prevention.com, September 15, 2009, and December 2019
The Good, the Bad, the Ugly, screenplay by Furio Scarpelli, directed and produced by Sergio Leeme
CL Barnhart, *The American College Dictionary,* (NY: Random House, 1961).
I Have Learned, KG Bush, Hidden Strengths
Helpguide.org/mental/mental_emotional_healthhtm
U.S. Army
Abigail Shiner, Artist Contributor

After much introspection and evaluation, I am finding myself not wanting to close down shop. Maybe most writers (especially us old*er* new writers) always feel that "there is more to say" (or write!). With humor and humility and in the grandest of ways, I hope this book has touched or will touch someone in need of strengthening their mental and physical health.

My wish for all of *y'all*—a good ole southern word that might go viral—would be for each of you to find your happy place soon. If you are already living in your happy place, please repair the daily damages and try to maintain your happy. Hold your middle ground. And finally, don't worry and be happy.

Much love to all.

About the Author

Sharla King was inspired to write this book by some previous health issues that she survived three times and by fifty-plus years of experience in real-time counseling experiences. Mostly, Sharla has gained counseling knowledge from working with people and her love of people and the desire to always help people.